Middle Manager Manifesto

Tools To Survive And Thrive In The World Of Work

By J Cleveland Payne

Copyright © 2024 J Cleveland Payne

All rights reserved.

ISBN: 9798326964922

Acknowledgements

I owe a great deal of gratitude to several individuals who have been instrumental in the inspiration for this book about middle managers.

To Johnsie, my civilian boss when I was in the Air Force, your leadership and willingness to learn from me have profoundly shaped my understanding of effective management. Your example of dedication and strength has been a guiding light.

To Joe, my radio boss, thank you for teaching me the power of communication and the importance of connecting with others. Your insights and experiences have enriched this book immeasurably.

To George, my boss in education, who is not an educator himself, your wisdom and guidance have been invaluable. Your ability to grit your teeth to make it look like a smile and just get things done is truly amazing and a huge inspiration for me to pursue this project.

To my wife, your unwavering support and encouragement have been the cornerstone of my career journey. Your patience and love have made this possible, and I am eternally grateful.

Thank you all for your contributions, which have been instrumental in bringing this book to life.

Dedication

For all the aspiring middle managers stepping into a world of complexity and opportunity, this book is dedicated to you. In a landscape where your roles are often misunderstood and undervalued, you will hold the keys to bridging strategy and execution, leadership, and teamwork. Your resilience, empathy, and innovative spirit are the quiet magic that drives organizations forward. Please find strength in these pages and remember that your contribution is significant and essential to the humanistic fabric of our working world.

Table of Contents

All Hail The Middle Managers 1

Effective Communication Skills 7

Time Management Techniques.................13

Conflict Resolution Strategies..................19

Team Building Activities 25

Performance Evaluation Methods 31

Decision-Making Frameworks 39

Delegation Skills.......................................47

Motivation Techniques..............................53

Leadership Styles And Adaptability 59

Feedback Mechanisms.............................65

Crisis Management Plans 71

Resource Management............................77

Networking and Relationship Building 83

Continuous Learning and Development ..91

So, What Do You Do Now? 97

Research, Sources, and A Little AI Magic 103

About The Author....................................115

All Hail The Middle Managers

The Positions May Be Diminishing, But The Roles Are More Important Than Ever

Middle management has long been considered the backbone of businesses and corporations, acting as the crucial link between the strategic vision of upper management and the operational execution by frontline employees. These managers are indispensable in translating corporate strategies into actionable plans, fostering team cohesion, and ensuring that day-to-day operations align with the company's goals. Despite their critical functions, the role of middle managers is increasingly under scrutiny in the modern work age. With advancements in technology, the rise of agile organizational structures, and a growing emphasis on flattening hierarchies, the days of middle managers might seem numbered.

The importance of middle managers cannot be overstated. They are the ones who bridge the gap between the top executives and the employees who carry out the everyday tasks. By doing so, they ensure that the vision and strategies devised by the company's upper echelons are effectively communicated and implemented on the ground. Middle managers also play a pivotal role in employee engagement, helping to attract, retain, and motivate talent within the organization. They are often the go-to individuals for problem-solving and decision-making, providing guidance and support to their teams. This dual function of managing upwards and downwards places middle managers at the heart of any successful business operation.

However, the traditional role of middle managers is facing challenges. In an era where agility and rapid response are prized, the layers of management can sometimes be seen as impediments to swift decision-making and innovation. Companies are increasingly adopting flatter organizational structures, which aim to reduce the number of hierarchical levels and promote a more direct line of communication between all employees. Additionally, the automation of routine tasks and the use of sophisticated data analytics tools are shifting the focus away from human intermediaries towards technology-driven solutions. These trends suggest a decline in the need for traditional middle management roles.

Despite these challenges, there is a story of hope for those who occupy or aspire to middle management positions. The evolving business landscape is not just about eliminating roles but about transforming them. Middle managers who can adapt to these changes, embrace new technologies, and develop a broader skill set will not only survive but also thrive in the new world of work. Those who can leverage their unique position to drive innovation, champion change, and mentor future leaders will remain invaluable to their organizations.

One of the critical ways middle managers can maintain their relevance is by focusing on continuous learning and development. By staying abreast of industry trends, acquiring new skills, and embracing lifelong learning, middle managers can enhance their ability to contribute strategically to their organizations. This proactive approach prepares them for the evolving demands of their role and positions them as potential candidates for upper management. The journey from middle to upper management is often paved with a commitment to personal and professional growth, demonstrating the ability to lead effectively and drive positive change within the organization.

Moreover, middle managers have a unique opportunity to shape the future leaders of their companies. By acting as mentors and coaches, they can impart valuable knowledge and skills to their team members, fostering a culture of continuous improvement and development. This mentoring role is crucial for building a solid leadership pipeline within the organization. By investing in the growth of their employees, middle managers not only enhance the performance of their teams but also contribute to the company's long-term success. This dual focus on personal growth and the development of others can create a lasting impact, ensuring that the organization remains competitive and innovative.

As middle managers navigate the complexities of their roles, it is essential to recognize the tools and strategies that can help them succeed. The following chapters of this book will present 14 essential tools designed to equip middle managers with the skills and knowledge they need to excel. These tools, collectively referred to as 'Tools To Survive And Thrive In The World Of Work,' cover various topics, including effective communication, time management, conflict resolution, and strategic thinking. Each tool is aimed at helping middle managers enhance their performance, drive team success, and achieve their career goals.

While the role of middle managers is evolving, it remains a vital part of organizational success. Middle managers can ensure their relevance and value in the modern workplace by embracing change, focusing on continuous learning, and leveraging their unique position to mentor and develop others. The journey ahead may be challenging, but with the right tools and mindset, middle managers can survive and thrive, shaping the future of their organizations and their careers. The 14 tools presented in this book are designed to guide you through this journey, providing practical insights and strategies to help you succeed, no matter where your current station in business may be.

Tool #1

Effective Communication Skills

Developing Clear And Concise Communication Channels Is Essential For Bridging Gaps Between Upper Management And Team Members

Effective communication skills are the cornerstone of successful middle management. In the complex organizational structures of modern businesses, middle managers often find themselves acting as the vital link between upper management and team members. This unique position requires a high level of communication proficiency to ensure that strategies, goals, and expectations are clearly understood by everyone involved. Clear and concise communication channels are beneficial and essential for bridging the gaps that can often exist between different levels of an organization.

One of the primary responsibilities of a middle manager is to translate the vision and directives of upper management into actionable tasks for their team. This process can be challenging if the communication is not handled effectively. Upper management typically operates strategically, focusing on long-term goals and broader company objectives. Their communication often contains high-level directives that must be broken down into specific, manageable tasks for the team. As a middle manager, your ability to distill complex information into clear, actionable steps is crucial. This ensures that your team understands what needs to be done, why it is essential, and how it fits into the larger organizational picture.

Miscommunication can lead to confusion, wasted effort, and frustration among team members. When directives are unclear, employees may spend valuable time interpreting what is expected of them, which can lead to mistakes and reduced productivity. Conversely, clear communication helps align everyone's efforts, ensuring that all team members work towards the same goals with a shared understanding of their roles and responsibilities. This alignment boosts efficiency and fosters a sense of purpose and motivation within the team.

Effective communication is also critical when it comes to feedback and performance evaluation. Constructive feedback is a powerful tool for professional growth and development, but its effectiveness depends largely on how it is communicated. Feedback should be specific, focused on behaviors and outcomes, and delivered in a supportive and encouraging way. By developing your skills in giving and receiving feedback, you can create a culture of continuous improvement and mutual respect within your team.

Another key aspect of communication for middle managers is the ability to listen actively. Listening is not just about hearing words but understanding the underlying messages and emotions. Active listening involves paying full attention to the speaker, asking clarifying questions, and providing thoughtful responses. This practice helps to build trust and rapport with team members, making them feel valued and understood. Employees who feel heard are more likely to be engaged, motivated, and committed to their work.

Open and transparent communication is essential for building trust within the team. Transparency involves sharing information openly and honestly, whether it is good news or bad. Keeping team members informed about changes, challenges, and successes helps to create a sense of stability and trust. When employees feel that they are kept in the loop and that their manager is honest and forthcoming, they are more likely to trust their leadership and be more cooperative and productive.

Middle managers must also navigate the delicate balance of advocating for their team while aligning with upper management's objectives. This requires a diplomatic communication style that respects the perspectives and interests of both parties. When advocating for your team, clearly and professionally presenting their needs and concerns is as important as providing evidence and examples to support your points. At the same time, you must communicate the rationale behind upper management's decisions to your team, helping them understand and buy into the larger strategic goals.

Technology can be a valuable ally in enhancing communication within teams. Project management software, instant messaging platforms, and video conferencing can facilitate real-time communication and collaboration, especially in remote or distributed teams. However, it is vital to use these tools effectively, ensuring that they enhance rather than hinder communication. For example, while instant messaging can be great for quick questions and updates, more complex or sensitive discussions might be better suited for face-to-face meetings or video calls.

Regular team meetings are another essential component of effective communication. These meetings provide an opportunity to share updates, discuss challenges, and plan for the future. They should be well-structured and focused, with clear agendas and objectives. Encouraging participation and open dialogue during these meetings helps to ensure that everyone has a voice and that diverse perspectives are considered.

In addition to formal communication channels, informal interactions can also play a significant role in building solid relationships within the team. Taking the time to engage with team members personally, whether through casual conversations, team-building activities, or social events, can help strengthen bonds and create a positive team culture. These informal interactions make it easier to address issues and resolve conflicts when they arise.

To bridge the gaps between upper management and team members, practical communication skills are essential for middle managers. Middle managers can create a cohesive and productive team environment by developing clear and concise communication, practicing active listening, providing constructive feedback, and fostering open and transparent communication. Embracing technology, conducting regular team meetings, and engaging in informal interactions further enhance communication and build stronger relationships within the team. These skills and practices not only improve the day-to-day functioning of the team but also contribute to the overall success and growth of the organization.

Tool #2

Time Management Techniques

Mastering Time Management Helps In Prioritizing Tasks And Ensuring Deadlines Are Met Without Unnecessary Stress

For modern business organizations and workplaces, time management is an indispensable skill for middle managers. As the linchpin between upper management and frontline employees, middle managers juggle multitudes of tasks daily. Mastering time management is not merely about getting more done in less time; it's about prioritizing effectively, meeting deadlines, and maintaining a sense of calm and control amidst the chaos. The art of managing time well can transform the way you work, enhancing productivity and reducing stress.

Understanding where your time goes is the first step toward effective time management. Conducting a time audit can be revealing. Tracking your activities over a week can identify patterns and pinpoint areas where time is wasted. This awareness is crucial for making informed decisions about allocating your time more effectively. For instance, you might discover that a significant portion of your day is consumed by emails and meetings, leaving little time for strategic thinking or essential projects. With this insight, you can begin to restructure your schedule, setting aside dedicated blocks of time for different types of work.

Once you have a clear picture of your current time usage, the next step is to prioritize tasks. Not all tasks are created equal; some significantly impact your goals and your team's success more than others. The Eisenhower Matrix is a helpful tool for categorizing tasks based on urgency and importance. Tasks that are urgent and important should be tackled immediately, while those that are important but not urgent can be scheduled for later. Tasks that are urgent but not important might be delegated, and those that are neither urgent nor important can often be eliminated. This approach helps ensure that you focus your energy on what truly matters.

Another critical aspect of time management is setting clear and achievable goals. These goals should be Specific, Measurable, Achievable, Relevant, and Time-bound (SMART). With clearly defined goals, you create a roadmap that guides your daily activities and decisions. For example, if one of your goals is to improve team performance, you might set specific milestones, such as increasing productivity by 10% over the next quarter. Breaking down larger goals into smaller, manageable tasks makes them less daunting and more attainable.

Effective planning is also essential. At the beginning of each week, take some time to plan out your schedule. Identify your most important tasks and allocate time for them first. This practice, often called "time blocking," involves dedicating specific parts of your day to particular activities. You can work more efficiently and with greater focus by reserving uninterrupted time for high-priority tasks. Reviewing and adjusting your plan at the end of each day is helpful, as it allows you to reflect on what worked well and what didn't. This continuous improvement mindset helps you refine your approach over time.

Interruptions and distractions are inevitable, but you can find ways to manage them. Creating a workspace that minimizes distractions is a good start. This might mean setting up in a quiet area, turning off notifications, or using tools like noise-canceling headphones. Additionally, learning to say no is an important skill. Getting pulled into meetings or tasks that aren't aligned with your priorities is easy, so do what you can to make sure this does not happen. Politely decline or delegate these requests when you can free up valuable time for more critical work.

Delegation is a powerful time management strategy that needs to be more utilized. As a middle manager, you don't have to do everything yourself. Delegating tasks to team members gives you more free time, empowers your team, and helps them develop new skills. When delegating, it's essential to be clear about expectations and provide the necessary resources and support. Trust your team to take ownership of their tasks and provide feedback to help them grow.

Technology can also be a great ally in managing your time more effectively. Numerous tools and apps are designed to help with scheduling, task management, and communication. Project management software like Asana or Trello can help you organize tasks and track progress. Calendar apps can be used to block time for focused work, while communication tools like Slack or Microsoft Teams can streamline interactions and reduce the time spent on emails.

In addition to these practical strategies, it's important to take care of yourself. Time management is not just about work; it's also about maintaining a healthy work-life balance. Make sure to carve out time for breaks and relaxation. Taking short breaks throughout the day can help you stay focused and energized. Additionally, finding time for exercise, hobbies, and spending time with loved ones is crucial for your overall well-being. A balanced approach to time management helps prevent burnout and keeps you motivated. Remember, your well-being is just as important as your work. Taking care of yourself is a key part of effective time management.

Mastering time management is a continuous process of learning and adapting. By understanding where your time goes, prioritizing tasks, setting clear goals, and using effective planning techniques, you can take control of your schedule and work more efficiently. Managing interruptions, delegating tasks, leveraging technology, and taking care of yourself are all important components of a comprehensive time management strategy. As a middle manager, these skills will not only help you meet deadlines and achieve your goals but also reduce stress and improve your overall quality of life. Embracing these techniques will enable you to navigate the complexities of your role with greater ease and confidence, ultimately leading to a more productive and fulfilling career. You'll feel more at ease and less overwhelmed as you gain the tools to manage your time effectively.

Tool #3

Conflict Resolution Strategies

Equipping Managers With Conflict Resolution Tools Ensures A Harmonious Workplace And Prevents Small Issues From Escalating

Conflict in the workplace is inevitable. Differences in opinions, work styles, and personalities can lead to disagreements and tensions among team members. For middle managers, effectively managing and resolving these conflicts is crucial to maintaining a harmonious and productive work environment. Equipping managers with conflict resolution tools ensures a peaceful workplace and
prevents small issues from escalating into larger, more disruptive problems.

The first step in effective conflict resolution is to address the conflict promptly. Ignoring conflicts or hoping they will resolve themselves is rarely effective. Instead, managers should acknowledge the problem as soon as it arises. This proactive approach shows team members that their concerns are taken seriously and that the manager is committed to resolving them. Early addressing of conflicts prevents them from festering and potentially damaging team dynamics.

Understanding the root cause of the conflict is essential. Often, the issue that surfaces is just a symptom of a deeper underlying problem. By gathering information and listening to all parties involved, a manager can clarify the issues causing the conflict. This step involves active listening, where the manager must pay close attention to what each party is saying without interrupting or passing judgment. Asking open-ended questions can help uncover the true nature of the conflict and ensure that all perspectives are considered.

Once the issues have been clarified, it is essential to bring the involved parties together to discuss the conflict. This meeting should be conducted in a neutral and safe environment where everyone feels comfortable expressing their views. The manager's role is to facilitate the conversation, ensuring it remains constructive and focused on finding a resolution. Encouraging open and honest communication helps to build trust and shows that the manager values each team member's input.

During the discussion, focusing on the problem rather than personal attacks is crucial. Helping team members understand the impact of the conflict on the team's goals and productivity can shift the focus from individual grievances to collective outcomes. The manager should guide the conversation towards identifying common ground and mutually acceptable solutions. This collaborative approach fosters a sense of teamwork and shared responsibility for resolving the conflict.

Creating an open-door policy is another effective strategy for managing conflicts. When team members know they can approach their manager with concerns, they are more likely to communicate issues before they escalate, not after. This policy promotes transparency and trust within the team. Managers should encourage employees to voice their concerns and provide reassurance that their issues will be handled confidentially and respectfully.

In some cases, conflicts may arise from misunderstandings or miscommunications. Clarifying expectations and ensuring all team members are on the same page can help prevent many conflicts. Regular team meetings and clear communication channels are essential. Managers should ensure that team members understand their roles, responsibilities, and the objectives of their tasks. This clarity reduces the likelihood of conflicts arising from confusion or unmet expectations.

There are times when conflicts cannot be resolved through discussion alone. In such cases, bringing in a neutral third party, such as a mediator, can be beneficial. A mediator can facilitate the conversation and help the parties involved reach a fair and unbiased resolution. This approach is handy when emotions run high, or the conflict involves deeply entrenched positions.

Managers should also focus on developing their conflict management skills continuously. Training programs and workshops on conflict resolution can provide valuable tools and techniques. These programs often cover various strategies, such as negotiation, mediation, and problem-solving, which can be applied in different conflict scenarios. By enhancing their skills, managers can handle conflicts more effectively and confidently.

In addition to resolving conflicts, managers should strive to create a work environment that minimizes conflicts. Fostering a positive and inclusive team culture where diversity is respected and valued can reduce the likelihood of conflicts. Encouraging collaboration and teamwork, recognizing and rewarding positive behaviors, and providing opportunities for team-building activities can strengthen team cohesion and ease tensions.

Lastly, managers need to reflect on and learn from each conflict resolution experience. Evaluating what worked well and what could be improved helps managers refine their approach for future conflicts. Seeking feedback from team members involved in the conflict can also provide valuable insights and foster a culture of continuous improvement.

Conflict resolution is a vital skill that can make or break a career for middle managers. Managers can maintain a harmonious workplace by addressing conflicts promptly, understanding their root causes, facilitating open communication, and focusing on collaborative solutions. Equipping managers with practical conflict resolution tools ensures a peaceful work environment and prevents minor issues from escalating into more significant problems. Creating an open and transparent culture, continuously developing conflict management skills, and fostering a positive team environment are critical strategies for successful conflict resolution. By mastering these techniques, middle managers can enhance team dynamics, boost productivity, and create a more cohesive and motivated workforce.

Tool #4

Team Building Activities

Strong Teams Are Built Through Trust And Collaboration, Leading To Improved Productivity And Morale

Fostering a strong, cohesive team is one of the most critical tasks in middle management. A well-functioning team is the backbone of any successful organization, and team-building activities are essential in creating such teams. These activities are not just about having fun or taking a break from work; they are about building trust, encouraging collaboration, and ultimately improving productivity and morale.

Team building activities serve multiple purposes. They allow team members to interact outside the usual work environment, allowing them to see each other in a different light. This can break down barriers and foster a sense of camaraderie. When team members engage in activities together, they learn to rely on each other, which builds trust. Trust is a foundational element of any strong team because it creates a safe space for open communication and collaboration.

One of the primary benefits of team-building activities is improved communication. These activities often require team members to solve problems together, communicate effectively, and listen to each other. For instance, activities like escape rooms or treasure hunts require participants to share information and strategize as a group. These scenarios mirror real workplace situations where effective communication is crucial. By practicing these skills in a relaxed and fun setting, team members can transfer these abilities to their daily work, leading to better collaboration and fewer misunderstandings.

Another significant advantage of team building is the enhancement of collaboration. When people work together on tasks that require collective effort, they learn to appreciate each other's strengths and understand how to leverage these for the team's benefit. Activities that involve role-playing or team challenges can highlight the importance of each member's contribution and how they fit into the larger picture. This understanding fosters a collaborative spirit, where individuals are more willing to help each other and work towards common goals.

Team building activities also play a crucial role in boosting morale. They offer a break from the routine, allowing employees to relax and have fun. Employees who feel valued and enjoy their work environment are more motivated and engaged. This positive energy can significantly impact productivity. Happy employees are likelier to go the extra mile, be more creative, and contribute positively to the team's success.

Moreover, team building can help identify and nurture leadership qualities within the team. Natural leaders often emerge during these activities as they take the initiative and guide their peers. This can be an excellent opportunity for managers to observe and recognize potential leaders. Encouraging these individuals and providing them with further development opportunities can strengthen the team and ensure a pipeline of future leaders within the organization.

One common misconception about team building is that it requires elaborate planning and significant expense. While some activities can be costly, many practical team-building exercises are simple and inexpensive. For example, icebreaker questions at the beginning of meetings, short problem-solving challenges, or even a regular coffee break together can foster team spirit. The key is consistency and ensuring that these activities are inclusive and engaging for all team members.

Creating a culture of regular team building can also help in managing conflicts. When team members have strong relationships built on trust and understanding, they are more likely to address and resolve disputes amicably. Regular interactions through team-building activities create a sense of belonging and mutual respect, making it easier to navigate disagreements and find solutions that benefit everyone involved.

In addition to improving communication and collaboration, team-building activities can also enhance creativity and innovation. When team members are comfortable with each other, they are more likely to share ideas and think outside the box. Activities that challenge the team to develop creative solutions, such as brainstorming sessions or innovation workshops, can lead to new and innovative approaches to work tasks. This not only improves the team's performance but can also give the organization a competitive edge.

In implementing team-building activities, middle managers must be mindful of their team members' diverse needs and preferences. Activities should be chosen carefully to ensure they are inclusive and cater to different personalities and abilities. It's also important to debrief after each activity to discuss what was learned and how it can be applied to the workplace. This reflection helps reinforce and integrate the lessons learned into daily work practices.

Overall, team-building activities are a powerful tool for middle managers. They build trust, enhance communication and collaboration, boost morale, and can even identify future leaders within the team. Managers can create a more cohesive, productive, and motivated team by investing time and effort into regular team building. The positive effects of these activities extend beyond the immediate fun and camaraderie; they build a strong foundation for ongoing team success and organizational growth.

Indeed, the importance of team-building activities cannot be overstated. They are essential for creating strong, collaborative teams that are the cornerstone of any successful organization. Middle managers play a crucial role in facilitating these activities and ensuring that their teams reap the full benefits. By prioritizing team building, managers can foster an environment where trust, collaboration, and productivity thrive, leading to better outcomes for the team and the organization as a whole.

Tool #5

Performance Evaluation Methods

Regular And Fair Performance Evaluations Help In Recognizing Talent And Addressing Areas Of Improvement.

Performance evaluations are vital for employees and managers in the fast-paced business world. For middle managers, mastering the art of performance evaluations is essential. These evaluations are not just routine check-ins; they are opportunities to recognize talent, address areas of improvement, and foster professional growth. Performing regular and fair performance evaluations helps build a transparent, productive, and motivated workforce.

A well-structured performance evaluation process begins with clear expectations. Employees need to understand what is expected of them regarding productivity, quality of work, and professional conduct. This clarity helps in setting the foundation for evaluations. When employees know the benchmarks they must meet, they are more likely to align their efforts with organizational goals. Managers should communicate these expectations clearly at the beginning of the evaluation period and provide ongoing feedback to keep employees on track.

The frequency of performance evaluations can vary depending on the organization, but regular reviews are crucial. Annual reviews are common, but they should be supplemented with more frequent check-ins. Quarterly or bi-annual reviews allow for more timely feedback and adjustments. These regular evaluations help identify and address issues before they become significant problems. They also provide opportunities to recognize and reward achievements, boosting employee morale and motivation.

Fairness is a cornerstone of effective performance evaluations. Evaluations should be based on objective criteria and measurable outcomes to ensure fairness. Subjective opinions and biases can undermine the credibility of the evaluation process. Managers should use standardized evaluation forms and criteria to assess performance. These tools can include rating scales, specific performance indicators, and examples of expected behaviors. Using these standardized tools, managers can provide consistent and objective employee evaluations.

Gathering comprehensive feedback is another essential aspect of performance evaluations. While self-assessments allow employees to reflect on their own performance, peer reviews and 360-degree feedback provide additional perspectives. Peer reviews can highlight collaborative skills and teamwork, while 360-degree feedback involves input from colleagues, subordinates, and supervisors. This holistic approach helps get a well-rounded view of an employee's performance. However, it's important to manage the potential biases in peer reviews and ensure that feedback is constructive and focused on behaviors rather than personalities.

During the evaluation meeting, effective communication is vital. Managers should create a supportive environment where employees feel comfortable discussing their performance. This conversation should be a two-way dialogue, not just a top-down assessment. Employees should be encouraged to share their achievements, challenges, and goals. Active listening by the manager is crucial. Managers can provide more targeted and meaningful feedback by understanding the employee's perspective.

Recognizing achievements is a vital part of performance evaluations. Celebrating successes and acknowledging hard work can have a significant positive impact on employee morale. Recognition can take many forms, from verbal praise and written commendations to more tangible rewards like bonuses or promotions. Highlighting achievements motivates the individual and sets a positive example for the rest of the team.

Addressing areas of improvement is equally important. Constructive feedback should be specific, actionable, and delivered in a supportive manner. Instead of simply pointing out shortcomings, managers should work with employees to develop improvement plans. These plans include setting specific goals, providing additional training, or offering mentorship. The focus should be on helping employees grow and succeed rather than simply criticizing their performance.

Development planning is a crucial component of performance evaluations. This involves setting future goals and identifying opportunities for professional growth. Managers should work with employees to set SMART goals – Specific, Measurable, Achievable, Relevant, and Time-bound. These goals provide a clear roadmap for the employee's development and align their efforts with the organization's strategic objectives. Regular follow-ups on these goals can help track progress and make necessary adjustments.

Documenting the evaluation process is essential for transparency and accountability. Detailed records of performance reviews, including notes from evaluation meetings, ratings, and feedback, should be maintained. This documentation helps track an employee's progress over time and provides a reference for future evaluations. It also ensures that the evaluation process is transparent and that decisions are based on documented evidence rather than subjective opinions.

In addition to formal evaluations, ongoing feedback is critical. Managers should provide regular feedback throughout the year, not just during scheduled evaluations. This continuous feedback helps keep employees aligned with their goals and address issues as they arise. It also creates a culture of open communication where feedback is seen as a normal part of the work process rather than a stressful event.

Training and support for managers conducting performance evaluations are essential. Organizations should provide training on effective evaluation techniques, communication skills, and bias management. This training helps managers conduct fair and constructive assessments that benefit employees and the organization. HR and senior leadership support can also provide managers with the resources and guidance to perform evaluations effectively.

Performance evaluations are a powerful tool for recognizing talent and addressing areas of improvement. By conducting regular and fair evaluations, middle managers can help their teams grow and succeed. These evaluations provide a structured way to celebrate achievements, identify development needs, and set future goals. They also foster a culture of continuous improvement and open communication. Mastering performance evaluation methods is essential for middle managers who want to build strong, motivated, high-performing teams.

Tool #6

Decision-Making Frameworks

Using Structured Decision-Making Processes Ensures That Choices Are Well-Considered And Beneficial For The Team

Making decisions is an everyday necessity for a modern middle manager. These decisions, whether minor or monumental, shape the direction and success of a team. Middle managers benefit immensely from employing structured decision-making frameworks to navigate this complex landscape. These frameworks ensure that choices are well-considered and align with the organization's overall goals, fostering beneficial outcomes for the team.

Structured decision-making processes provide a systematic approach to tackling problems and evaluating options. These frameworks are at the heart of breaking down complex decisions into manageable steps. This systematic approach helps managers avoid the pitfalls of rushed judgments and biases, ensuring that all relevant factors are considered. One widely recognized framework is the Cynefin framework, which categorizes decisions based on their context—simple, complicated, complex, and chaotic. Each category requires a different approach, helping managers tailor their decision-making process to the specific nature of the problem.

Managers can rely on best practices and established procedures in simple contexts with clear cause-and-effect relationships. These decisions require straightforward management and monitoring. The goal here is to sense, categorize, and respond. For example, routine operational decisions often fall into this category. By correctly classifying these decisions, managers can ensure they use the most efficient and effective methods available.

When dealing with complicated contexts where there might be multiple right answers, expertise becomes crucial. This scenario often involves analytical decision-making and thorough investigation. Managers gather data, analyze it, and use their knowledge to determine the best course of action. This might include consulting with experts or using detailed analytical tools. The structured approach ensures that decisions are backed by evidence and informed by those with the most relevant knowledge.

Complex contexts, on the other hand, involve unknowns and unpredictability. Here, patterns may emerge only in retrospect. Managers must probe, sense, and respond, experimenting and learning from the outcomes. This adaptive approach encourages innovation and allows teams to navigate uncertainty more effectively. By using frameworks that emphasize learning and adaptability, managers can confidently lead their teams through complex situations, knowing that they have a process to fall back on even when the path ahead is unclear.

Chaotic contexts require immediate action to establish order. Managers must act decisively to stabilize the situation and assess how to prevent future occurrences. This might involve crisis management techniques where the priority is to contain the chaos and restore normalcy quickly. Structured frameworks guide managers through these high-pressure situations, ensuring their actions are deliberate and aimed at stabilizing the environment as soon as possible.

The benefits of using structured decision-making frameworks extend beyond just making the right choices. These processes also foster transparency and accountability. When team members understand the rationale behind decisions, they are more likely to trust and support them. Transparency in decision-making involves documenting the process, the criteria considered, and the reasoning behind the final choice. This documentation not only helps in justifying decisions but also serves as a learning tool for future situations.

Involving the team in the decision-making process can also be highly beneficial. Collaborative decision-making frameworks encourage input from various stakeholders, ensuring that multiple perspectives are considered. This collective approach can lead to more innovative solutions and a stronger sense of ownership among team members. For instance, brainstorming sessions or decision matrices allow team members to contribute their insights, fostering a more inclusive and engaged work environment.

One practical approach to structured decision-making is the use of decision trees. These tools help managers visualize the different possible outcomes of a decision and the paths that lead to them. By mapping out the various options and their potential consequences, managers can better assess the risks and benefits of each choice. Decision trees are beneficial in scenarios with multiple variables and possible outcomes, providing a clear framework for evaluating each possibility.

Another effective method is the SWOT analysis, which involves evaluating the strengths, weaknesses, opportunities, and threats related to a decision. This structured approach helps managers comprehensively assess the internal and external factors that could impact the decision. By systematically analyzing these elements, managers can make more informed choices that leverage strengths, mitigate weaknesses, capitalize on opportunities, and guard against threats.

Scenario planning is also a valuable tool in the decision-making toolkit. This approach involves developing different scenarios based on various assumptions about the future. By considering multiple potential futures, managers can prepare for various possible outcomes and develop robust strategies under different conditions. Scenario planning encourages strategic thinking and helps managers anticipate and respond to environmental changes.

Ultimately, using structured decision-making frameworks aims to enhance the quality of decisions and ensure they benefit the team and organization. These frameworks provide a disciplined approach that helps managers navigate the complexities of their roles with greater confidence and effectiveness. By relying on structured processes, managers can reduce the influence of biases, make more objective decisions, and create a more transparent and accountable decision-making environment.

Structured decision-making frameworks are invaluable tools for middle managers. They provide a systematic approach to tackling complex problems, ensure that decisions are well-considered and beneficial, and foster a culture of transparency and collaboration. By mastering these frameworks, middle managers can enhance their decision-making capabilities, lead their teams more effectively, and contribute to the overall success of their organizations.

Tool #7

Delegation Skills

Effective Delegation Empowers Team Members And Allows Managers To Focus On High-Level Strategic Tasks

Modern workplaces require effective delegation as a critical skill middle managers must possess. Delegation is not just about offloading tasks; it is about strategically assigning responsibilities to team members to enhance efficiency, foster professional growth, and allow managers to focus on higher-level strategic objectives. Mastering the art of delegation can transform a team's productivity and morale, making it a cornerstone of successful management.

Delegation begins with a clear understanding of the tasks and the capabilities of the team members. Managers must know their team's strengths, weaknesses, and development areas. This knowledge enables them to match tasks with the right individuals, ensuring that the work is done efficiently and effectively. When tasks are aligned with an employee's skills and interests, it not only improves the quality of the output but also boosts the employee's engagement and job satisfaction. This alignment is crucial for fostering a sense of ownership and responsibility among team members.

One of the primary benefits of effective delegation is that it empowers team members. When employees are entrusted with significant responsibilities, they feel valued and trusted. This empowerment leads to increased motivation and commitment to their work. Moreover, delegation allows team members to develop new skills and gain experience in different areas. This growth benefits both the individual and the organization, as it creates a more versatile and capable workforce.

For managers, effective delegation is essential for focusing on high-level strategic tasks. By entrusting team members with specific responsibilities, managers can free up their time to concentrate on planning, decision-making, and other critical activities that require their expertise. This shift in focus allows managers to drive the strategic direction of the team and the organization, ensuring that long-term goals are met while day-to-day operations run smoothly.

However, the delegation of tasks does have challenges. One common obstacle is the fear of losing control. Some managers worry that delegated tasks will not be completed to the required standard. It is crucial to establish clear expectations and provide the necessary resources and support to overcome this outcome. Setting specific, measurable, achievable, relevant, and time-bound (SMART) goals for delegated tasks helps ensure everyone is on the same page. Regular check-ins and feedback sessions are also crucial. These interactions allow managers to monitor progress, promptly address issues, and provide guidance and support as needed.

Another challenge is selecting the right tasks to delegate. Not all tasks are suitable for delegation. Managers should delegate tasks that are time-consuming but do not necessarily require their expertise. Routine tasks, administrative duties, and projects that offer learning opportunities for team members are ideal candidates for delegation. On the other hand, tasks that involve confidential information, critical decision-making, or require the manager's unique skills should generally remain under the manager's direct control.

Building a culture of trust is fundamental to successful delegation. Trust is a two-way street. Managers must trust their team members to take on responsibilities and perform tasks effectively. Similarly, employees need to trust that their managers will provide the support and guidance they need to succeed. This trust can be nurtured through open communication, transparency, and a supportive environment. When team members feel trusted and supported, they are more likely to take initiative, seek solutions, and go the extra mile.

Effective communication is at the heart of successful delegation. Managers must clearly articulate delegated tasks' objectives, expectations, and deadlines. It is also important to outline the boundaries of the delegated authority, so team members know the extent of their decision-making power. Clear communication reduces the risk of misunderstandings and ensures everyone is working towards the same goals. Additionally, fostering an environment where team members feel comfortable asking questions and seeking clarification can prevent potential issues and enhance the quality of the work.

Delegation also involves providing feedback. Constructive feedback helps team members understand what they are doing well and where to improve. This feedback should be specific, actionable, and delivered in a way that encourages growth and learning. Celebrating successes and acknowledging efforts can further motivate employees and reinforce positive behaviors. Constructive feedback and recognition create a positive feedback loop that enhances performance and development.

Training and development play a crucial role in effective delegation. Providing team members with the necessary training equips them with the skills and knowledge to handle delegated tasks confidently and competently. Investing in their development shows that the organization values their growth and is willing to support their career progression. This investment can increase employee retention and a more skilled and capable team.

Effective delegation is a powerful tool for middle managers. It empowers team members, fosters professional growth, and allows managers to focus on strategic tasks. Managers can delegate tasks effectively and drive their teams toward success by understanding their strengths and capabilities, communicating clearly, building trust, and providing support and feedback. Mastering delegation is not just about improving efficiency; it is about creating a positive and productive work environment where everyone can thrive. As middle managers embrace and refine their delegation skills, they will find themselves leading more engaged, motivated, and high-performing teams, ultimately contributing to the overall success of their organization.

Tool #8

Motivation Techniques

Keeping The Team Motivated Ensures High Performance And Job Satisfaction

Whether you are deep into corporate management or brought in to help manage a mom-and-pop operation, keeping a team motivated is paramount. Motivation drives performance, fosters job satisfaction, and cultivates an environment where employees feel valued and engaged. For middle managers, mastering motivational techniques is a critical component of leadership that can significantly influence the success and cohesion of their teams.

Motivation begins with understanding what drives each team member. People are motivated by different factors, and recognizing these can help managers tailor their approach. Financial incentives may drive some employees, while others find fulfillment in professional growth opportunities or recognition for their efforts. Acknowledging and addressing these individual drivers can create a more motivated and productive team.

Effective communication is at the heart of motivation. Managers should regularly engage with their team members to give instructions, listen, and understand their concerns, aspirations, and feedback. Open communication fosters a sense of belonging and shows employees that their opinions matter. When team members feel heard and valued, their commitment to their work and the organization increases. Regular one-on-one meetings can provide a platform for such interactions, allowing managers to build stronger relationships and address issues before they escalate.

Setting clear and attainable goals is another crucial motivational technique. Goals provide direction and purpose, helping employees understand what is expected of them and how their efforts contribute to the organization's success. When setting goals, it's essential to ensure they are Specific, Measurable, Achievable, Relevant, and Time-bound (SMART). Clear goals give employees a sense of direction and accomplishment as they work towards achieving them. Moreover, breaking down larger goals into smaller, manageable tasks can keep employees from feeling overwhelmed and motivated.

Recognition and rewards play a significant role in maintaining motivation. Recognizing employees for their hard work and achievements can boost morale and encourage a culture of excellence. This recognition can take various forms, from a simple thank-you note or public acknowledgment during team meetings to tangible rewards like bonuses or promotions. Celebrating milestones and successes, no matter how small, reinforces positive behavior and motivates employees to continue performing at their best. Recognition must be genuine and specific, highlighting what the employee did well and why it was valuable to the team and organization.

Creating opportunities for professional development is another powerful motivator. Offering training programs, workshops, and opportunities for career advancement shows employees that the organization is invested in their growth. When employees see a clear path for advancement and feel they are gaining valuable skills, they are more likely to be engaged and motivated. Encouraging continuous learning not only enhances the individual's capabilities but also brings new skills and ideas into the team, driving innovation and improvement.

Autonomy is a significant driver of motivation. Allowing employees the freedom to make decisions and take ownership of their work fosters a sense of responsibility and trust. Micromanaging can stifle creativity and reduce motivation, whereas giving employees the autonomy to approach tasks their way can boost their confidence and satisfaction. This autonomy should come with clear expectations and support, ensuring employees have the resources and guidance they need to succeed.

Building a positive team culture is essential for sustaining motivation. A supportive and collaborative environment where team members feel connected and valued can significantly enhance motivation. Team-building activities, social events, and regular team meetings can strengthen relationships and foster a sense of community. Employees who enjoy working together and feel part of a cohesive team naturally improve their motivation and performance.

Addressing and resolving conflicts promptly is also crucial. Unresolved conflicts can lead to a toxic work environment, reducing motivation and productivity. Managers should proactively identify and address issues, fostering an open environment where team members feel comfortable voicing their concerns. Effective conflict resolution maintains a positive work environment and shows employees that the manager is committed to their well-being and the overall harmony of the team.

Work-life balance is another critical aspect of motivation. Encouraging employees to take breaks, use their vacation days, and maintain a healthy balance between work and personal life can prevent burnout and keep motivation levels high. Flexible work arrangements can also improve work-life balance and increase job satisfaction.

Finally, leading by example is a powerful motivational technique. Managers who demonstrate commitment, enthusiasm, and a positive attitude can inspire their team to adopt the same approach. Being a role model regarding work ethic, communication, and problem-solving sets a standard for the team and fosters a culture of excellence.

Keeping a team motivated is an ongoing process that requires a combination of strategies tailored to the needs and preferences of each team member. By fostering open communication, setting clear goals, recognizing and rewarding achievements, providing development opportunities, granting autonomy, building a positive culture, addressing conflicts, ensuring work-life balance, and leading by example, middle managers can create an environment where employees are motivated to perform at their best and find satisfaction in their work. These techniques enhance individual performance and contribute to the overall success and cohesion of the team and organization.

Tool #9

Leadership Styles And Adaptability

Understanding Different Leadership Styles And Adapting Them To Various Situations Helps In Managing Diverse Teams

Adapting one's leadership style to various situations is a crucial skill for middle managers in the ever-evolving landscape of modern business. Leadership is not a one-size-fits-all endeavor; it requires a nuanced understanding of different approaches and the flexibility to apply the right style at the right time. This adaptability is essential when managing diverse teams, where cultural differences, individual personalities, and varying experience levels come into play.

Understanding different leadership styles begins with self-awareness. Managers must first recognize their default leadership tendencies. Are they naturally more authoritative, preferring to set clear expectations and maintain tight control over processes? Or do they lean towards a more democratic style, seeking input and consensus from their team members? They may be drawn to a transformational approach, inspiring and motivating their team towards a shared vision. By understanding their inherent style, managers can better assess how to adapt their approach to suit different situations and team dynamics.

Assessing the situation is the next critical step. Different contexts call for different leadership styles. For instance, a more directive approach may be necessary in times of crisis or when quick decisions are needed. This involves providing clear instructions and making swift decisions to steer the team through turbulent waters. On the other hand, when working on a complex project that requires creativity and collaboration, a more participative style might be beneficial. This approach encourages team members to contribute their ideas and fosters a sense of ownership and engagement.

Adapting to the team is equally important. Each team member brings unique strengths, weaknesses, and preferences that a middle manager must evaluate to utilize effectively. Savvy middle managers understand the value of tailoring their leadership style to meet the needs of their team members. For example, new employees or those lacking confidence may benefit from a supportive and coaching style, where the manager provides guidance, encouragement, and opportunities for skill development. Conversely, experienced and highly skilled team members may thrive under a delegative style, where they can take ownership of their work and make decisions independently.

Balancing flexibility and consistency is a delicate dance that middle managers must master. While adaptability is crucial, it is also essential to maintain a consistent approach to certain core principles and values. This consistency helps build trust and reliability within the team. Employees must know that while the manager may adapt their style to different situations, they will consistently uphold the team's values and provide a stable and supportive environment.

Developing leadership skills is an ongoing journey. Managers must continuously seek opportunities to learn and grow. One can effectively achieve this as a manager through formal training programs, mentorship, and self-reflection. Additionally, seeking feedback from team members and peers can provide valuable insights into how one's leadership style is perceived and where there may be room for improvement. Embracing a continuous improvement mindset enhances a manager's effectiveness and sets a positive example for the team.

Cultural awareness plays a significant role in managing diverse teams. Understanding and respecting cultural differences can significantly enhance a manager's ability to lead effectively. This involves managers being mindful of different communication styles, attitudes towards authority, and varying expectations regarding work-life balance. By demonstrating cultural sensitivity and adapting their leadership approach, managers can create an inclusive environment where all team members feel valued and respected.

Collaborative leadership is another essential aspect of adaptability. This style emphasizes teamwork, shared decision-making, and collective responsibility. In today's interconnected world, collaboration is often the key to innovation and success. By fostering a collaborative culture, middle managers can harness their team's diverse talents and perspectives, leading to more creative solutions and better overall performance.

Navigating the flexibility of situational leadership involves understanding team members' readiness and development levels. Situational leadership theory suggests that managers should adjust their style based on the competence and commitment of their employees. For instance, a new hire with limited experience may require a more directive approach, clear instructions, and close supervision. As they gain confidence and skills, the manager can gradually shift to a more delegative style, allowing for greater autonomy and responsibility.

In addition to situational factors, the organizational culture and goals must influence a manager's leadership approach. Aligning one's style with the broader organizational values and objectives ensures coherence and reinforces a unified direction. For example, a transformational leadership style that encourages experimentation and embraces change may be most effective in a company prioritizing innovation and agility.

Ultimately, adapting leadership styles aims to enhance team performance and job satisfaction. When managers are adept at adjusting their approach to meet the needs of their team and the demands of the situation, they create an environment where employees are motivated, engaged, and empowered to excel. This adaptability drives better results and contributes to a positive and dynamic workplace culture.

Possessing the ability to understand and adapt different leadership styles is a vital skill for middle managers. By being self-aware, assessing situations accurately, and tailoring their approach to the unique needs of their team, managers can navigate the complexities of modern leadership with confidence and effectiveness. This adaptability, combined with a commitment to continuous learning and cultural awareness, positions middle managers to lead their teams to success in an ever-changing business landscape.

Tool #10

Feedback Mechanisms

Constructive Feedback Fosters Growth And Improvement, Both For The Team And The Manager.

Feedback is the lifeblood of professional growth and development. For middle managers, mastering the art of providing and receiving constructive feedback is crucial for fostering an environment of continuous improvement and high performance. Constructive feedback is not merely a tool for correction; it is a pathway to building stronger relationships, enhancing team dynamics, and driving personal and organizational growth.

The foundation of adequate and effective feedback mechanisms lies in establishing a culture of continuous feedback within the team. This culture promotes open communication and encourages team members to view feedback as a regular and expected part of their professional interactions. When feedback is normalized, it reduces anxiety and resistance, making it easier for employees to accept and act upon it. For managers, this means providing regular, thoughtful feedback rather than waiting for formal performance reviews. By doing so, managers can address issues promptly and recognize achievements in real time, fostering a more responsive and agile team environment.

Constructive feedback should always be specific and focused on behaviors rather than personal attributes. This approach helps to keep the feedback objective and actionable. For instance, instead of saying, "You need to be more professional," a manager might say, "In our last meeting, you interrupted several times, which disrupted the flow of conversation. Let's work on allowing others to finish speaking before you share your thoughts." This specificity clarifies the issue and provides a clear path for improvement. Employees are more likely to respond positively to tangible and clearly related feedback to their actions.

Another critical aspect of providing constructive feedback is timing. Manager feedback should be given as close to the event as possible to ensure that it is relevant and fresh in the minds of both the giver and the receiver. This immediacy helps address behaviors before they become ingrained and more difficult to change. However, managers should also be mindful of the context and the individual's emotional state. Providing feedback during high-stress moments or in public settings can be counterproductive. A private, calm, and supportive setting is ideal for these discussions.

The delivery of feedback is as important as its content. A growth mindset approach can significantly affect how feedback is received. This involves managers framing feedback to emphasize development and learning rather than criticism. For example, highlighting how a particular skill or behavior can be improved to achieve better results can be more motivating than focusing solely on what was done wrong. Encouraging employees to view feedback as an opportunity for growth helps to cultivate a positive and proactive attitude towards improvement.

Active listening is a vital component of the feedback process. When providing feedback, managers should ensure that it is a two-way conversation. This means actively listening to the employee's perspective, asking open-ended questions, and encouraging them to express their thoughts and feelings. This dialogue helps understand the root causes of certain behaviors and makes the employee feel heard and valued. Managers need to be empathetic and considerate, showing that they genuinely care about the employee's development and well-being.

For feedback to be truly effective, it must be followed by actionable steps and support. Managers should work with their team members to develop a clear action plan that outlines specific goals and the steps needed to achieve them. Providing resources, training, or mentorship can help employees improve their skills and performance. This ongoing support demonstrates the manager's commitment to their growth and ensures that feedback leads to tangible improvements.

Receiving feedback is equally important for managers. Encouraging a culture where feedback flows both ways helps managers understand their strengths and areas for improvement. It sets an example of humility and continuous learning, reinforcing the idea that everyone in the organization is on a journey of growth. Managers should regularly seek feedback from their team, peers, and superiors and be willing to act on it. This openness can enhance trust and respect within the team, creating a more cohesive and collaborative work environment.

In addition to individual feedback, fostering a culture of peer feedback can be highly beneficial. Peer feedback allows team members to learn from each other and provides diverse perspectives on their work. This practice can enhance collaboration and help identify blind spots that might be overlooked in hierarchical feedback structures. Managers should facilitate regular opportunities for peer feedback, such as team reviews or collaborative reflection sessions, and ensure that these interactions are constructive and focused on development.

Ultimately, the power of constructive feedback lies in its ability to drive growth and improvement. It means more explicit expectations, better communication, and enhanced performance for the team. For the manager, it fosters a deeper understanding of their team, stronger relationships, and more effective leadership. By establishing robust feedback mechanisms, middle managers can create an environment where continuous improvement is the norm, and both individuals and the organization can thrive.

Effective feedback mechanisms are essential for middle managers aiming to foster growth and improvement within their teams. When delivered effectively, constructive feedback can transform behaviors, enhance skills, and build stronger, more engaged teams. By creating a culture of continuous feedback, focusing on specific and actionable insights, and supporting employees through their development journey, managers can ensure that feedback serves as a catalyst for positive change and sustained success.

Tool #11

Crisis Management Plans

Being Prepared For Crises Ensures Swift And Effective Handling Of Unexpected Challenges

In the unpredictable world of business, crises are inevitable. Whether it's a sudden financial downturn, a critical system failure, or a public relations disaster, crises can emerge without warning and significantly impact an organization. For middle managers, having a well-thought-out crisis management plan is essential. Preparing for crises ensures they can be handled swiftly and effectively, minimizing damage and facilitating a quicker return to normal operations.

A crisis management plan starts with identifying potential crises. This involves conducting a thorough risk assessment to pinpoint vulnerabilities within the organization. These vulnerabilities could range from technological risks, such as cyber-attacks or system outages, to human resources issues, like key personnel departures or labor disputes. By understanding where the risks lie, managers can develop specific strategies to address each potential crisis. This proactive approach helps in mitigating risks before they escalate into full-blown crises.

Once potential crises are identified, the next step is to establish a crisis management team. This team should include individuals with diverse skills and knowledge relevant to the identified risks. The team's responsibilities include developing and implementing the crisis management plan and coordinating the response during an actual crisis. Clear roles and responsibilities should be assigned to ensure that everyone knows what is expected of them. Having a dedicated team allows for a more organized and efficient response, as team members can quickly spring into action when a crisis occurs.

Communication is a critical component of any crisis management plan. Clear and effective communication can distinguish between chaos and control during a crisis. It is essential to establish communication protocols that outline how information will be disseminated, who will be responsible for communicating with stakeholders, and what channels will be used. This includes internal and external communication with customers, the media, and other stakeholders. Ensuring that accurate and timely information is provided helps to maintain trust and transparency, which are crucial during times of uncertainty.

Training and drills are vital for ensuring that the crisis management plan can be executed effectively. Regular training sessions for the crisis management team and drills that simulate various crisis scenarios help keep everyone prepared. These exercises reinforce the plan and help identify any gaps or weaknesses that need to be addressed. By practicing the response to different types of crises, the team can build confidence and improve their ability to handle real-life situations.

A crucial aspect of crisis management is having a clear decision-making process. Decisions often need to be made quickly and under pressure during a crisis. Having a predefined decision-making framework can help you make informed and timely choices. This framework should outline the criteria for decision-making, who has the authority to make decisions, and how those decisions will be communicated and implemented. By establishing this process in advance, managers can avoid the paralysis that can occur when multiple stakeholders are involved, and time is of the essence.

Post-crisis evaluation is an often overlooked but essential part of crisis management. After the crisis has been resolved, it is crucial to conduct a thorough review to understand what went well and what could be improved. This evaluation should involve all members of the crisis management team and should consider both the effectiveness of the response and the impact of the crisis on the organization. Lessons learned from this evaluation can be used to update and improve the crisis management plan, preparing the organization for future crises.

One of the key benefits of being prepared for crises is that it enables swift and effective handling of unexpected challenges. When a crisis strikes, the ability to respond quickly can significantly reduce the impact. For example, if a company faces a sudden product recall, having a plan that includes steps for communicating with customers, managing logistics, and addressing the root cause can help contain the damage and restore customer confidence. Similarly, in the case of a cyber-attack, a well-prepared response that includes immediate measures to secure systems, notify affected parties, and begin recovery efforts can prevent further damage and expedite the return to normal operations.

In addition to minimizing damage, effective crisis management can enhance the organization's reputation. How a company handles a crisis can have a lasting impact on its public image. Demonstrating competence, transparency, and empathy during a crisis can strengthen stakeholder trust and loyalty. Conversely, a poorly managed crisis can lead to long-term reputational damage. Therefore, a robust crisis management plan is about mitigating risks, safeguarding, and potentially enhancing the organization's reputation.

For middle managers, having the ability to navigate crises successfully is a critical leadership skill. It involves planning, preparation, and the ability to remain calm and decisive under pressure. By fostering a culture of preparedness and resilience within their teams, middle managers can ensure that their organization is better equipped to handle whatever challenges come their way. This proactive approach not only helps in managing crises more effectively but also contributes to the overall stability and success of the organization.

Being prepared for crises through a well-developed crisis management plan is essential for middle managers. Identifying potential risks, establishing a crisis management team, ensuring clear communication, conducting regular training and drills, and having a defined decision-making process are all crucial components of effective crisis management. By being prepared, middle managers can handle unexpected challenges swiftly and effectively, minimizing damage and enhancing the organization's ability to recover and thrive.

Tool #12

Resource Management

Efficient Use Of Resources Maximizes Productivity And Reduces Waste

Resource management is a crucial aspect of middle management, often determining the success or failure of projects and initiatives. At its core, resource management involves the effective and efficient use of an organization's resources, including personnel, equipment, and finances. By optimizing these resources, managers can maximize productivity, reduce waste, and align their teams with the organization's strategic goals. This chapter delves into the importance of resource management and provides insights into how middle managers can excel in this critical area.

The first step in effective resource management is understanding the available resources and their capabilities. This involves a thorough inventory of the team's skills, tools, and the budget allocated for various projects. A clear understanding of these elements allows managers to allocate resources effectively, ensuring that each task is handled by the right person with the right tools and within budget constraints. This strategic allocation helps avoid bottlenecks and ensures that all team members are utilized to their fullest potential.

Efficient use of resources begins with planning. A well-thought-out plan includes detailed timelines, task assignments, and resource allocation. Managers should prioritize tasks based on their importance and deadlines, ensuring critical projects receive the necessary resources to meet their objectives. This planning phase also involves forecasting potential challenges and implementing contingency plans. By anticipating problems and preparing solutions, managers can mitigate risks and keep projects on track.

Communication is another critical component of resource management. Managers must communicate the resource plan to their team, ensuring everyone understands their roles, responsibilities, and available resources. Open lines of communication also allow team members to provide feedback and report any issues that may arise, enabling managers to make timely adjustments. Regular meetings and updates help keep everyone aligned and ensure resources are used efficiently.

Technology plays a significant role in modern resource management. Various software tools can help managers track resource utilization, monitor progress, and adjust allocations as needed. These tools provide real-time data and analytics, allowing managers to make informed decisions quickly. For instance, project management software can help assign tasks, set deadlines, and track the status of each project. Resource management tools can also highlight underutilized resources, enabling managers to redistribute them where they are needed most.

One of the primary goals of resource management is to minimize waste. This involves reducing physical waste and ensuring that human resources are not wasted. Idle time is a common issue in many organizations, where employees are not fully utilized due to poor planning or misallocation of tasks. Managers can minimize idle time and increase productivity by carefully scheduling tasks and ensuring that each team member has a steady stream of work. Additionally, regular performance reviews and feedback sessions can help identify any skills gaps or training needs, allowing managers to invest in their team's development and use their talents in better ways.

Resource management is also about balancing short-term demands with long-term goals. While meeting immediate project deadlines is essential, managers must also ensure that resources are developed and maintained for future needs. This might involve investing in new technology, upskilling employees, or improving processes to enhance efficiency. Managers can create a sustainable environment where resources are continuously optimized by taking a holistic view of resource management.

Collaboration is another critical aspect of resource management. Effective collaboration within the team and with other departments can lead to better resource utilization. Managers should encourage a culture of teamwork, where resources are shared, and support is provided across different functions. This collaborative approach helps pool resources and expertise, leading to more innovative solutions and efficient project execution.

Monitoring and evaluation are essential to ensure resource management strategies work as intended. Managers should regularly review resource utilization, track progress against goals, and make adjustments as necessary. Key performance indicators (KPIs) related to resource efficiency, such as utilization rates, project completion times, and cost savings, can provide valuable insights. By continuously monitoring these metrics, managers can identify areas for improvement and implement changes to enhance resource management practices.

Effective resource management not only maximizes productivity but also contributes to employee satisfaction. When resources are managed well, employees have the tools and support to perform their tasks efficiently. This reduces frustration, enhances job satisfaction, and fosters a positive work environment. Moreover, by recognizing and addressing the needs and potential of each team member, managers can build a motivated and engaged workforce.

Resource management is a vital function of middle management that directly impacts an organization's productivity and efficiency. Managers can ensure that their teams operate at peak performance by understanding and strategically allocating resources, communicating effectively, leveraging technology, minimizing waste, balancing short-term and long-term goals, fostering collaboration, and continuously monitoring and evaluating resource use. Efficient use of resources maximizes productivity and creates a sustainable and fulfilling work environment. Middle managers who excel in resource management are better equipped to lead their teams to success and contribute to their organization's overall goals.

Tool #13

Networking and Relationship Building

Building A Strong Professional Network Provides Support And Opens Up Opportunities For Collaboration And Growth

The role of a middle manager is multifaceted, and networking and relationship building are not just beneficial—they are essential. These activities extend beyond mere social interactions, forming the backbone of professional support, collaboration, and growth. By nurturing a robust professional network, middle managers can navigate challenges more effectively, unlock new opportunities, and foster a collaborative environment that drives organizational success.

At the heart of networking lies the principle of mutual benefit. Networking is about building genuine connections that offer support, share knowledge, and provide opportunities. For middle managers, this means developing relationships within and outside their organization. Internally, networking helps managers understand different perspectives, gain insights into other departments, and align their team's efforts with broader organizational goals. Externally, it connects them with peers in the industry, offering a platform to exchange best practices, discuss challenges, and explore potential collaborations.

One of the first steps in effective networking is recognizing its value. Networking should not be viewed as an obligatory task but as a strategic activity that can enhance personal and professional growth. This mindset shift is crucial for middle managers who often juggle multiple responsibilities and may find it challenging to allocate time for networking. By understanding the long-term benefits, such as increased access to information, enhanced problem-solving capabilities, and potential career advancements, managers can prioritize networking as an integral part of their professional development.

Building strong relationships begins with genuine interest and empathy. Managers should take the time to understand their colleagues' and peers' needs, goals, and challenges. This involves active listening and showing sincere interest in others' work and well-being. Empathy fosters trust, a fundamental component of any strong relationship. When team members and colleagues feel understood and valued, they are more likely to engage openly and collaborate effectively. This trust extends beyond immediate interactions, creating a supportive network that can be relied upon in times of need.

Consistency is another key element in relationship building. Regular interactions, whether through meetings, casual check-ins, or collaborative projects, help maintain and strengthen relationships. Managers need to be approachable and available, showing that they are willing to invest time and effort into their professional relationships. This ongoing engagement demonstrates commitment and reliability, reinforcing the bonds within the network.

Middle managers should also leverage various platforms and events to expand their network. Industry conferences, workshops, and seminars provide excellent opportunities to meet new people and learn about the latest trends and developments. Online platforms like LinkedIn are also valuable tools for connecting with professionals across the globe. By actively participating in these forums, managers can broaden their network and stay updated with industry advancements. Engaging in discussions, sharing insights, and contributing to the community can further enhance their professional visibility and credibility.

Another effective strategy is to focus on building a diverse network. A diverse network includes individuals with different backgrounds, experiences, and expertise. This diversity enriches the network with various perspectives and ideas, which can be invaluable in problem-solving and decision-making. For middle managers, this means connecting with people from different departments, industries, and professional levels. Such a network offers a wealth of knowledge and opens up opportunities for cross-functional collaborations and innovation.

Reciprocity is a cornerstone of effective networking. Successful relationships are built on the principle of give and take. Middle managers should seek to offer support and value to their network, whether through sharing knowledge, providing introductions, or offering assistance with challenges. This generosity fosters goodwill and strengthens the network, making support more likely to be reciprocated when needed. It's about creating a balance where both parties benefit from the relationship, leading to a more resilient and supportive network.

In addition to professional interactions, social engagements can also play a significant role in relationship building. Informal settings, such as team lunches, after-work gatherings, or casual coffee meetings, allow for more relaxed and personal interactions. These social bonds can enhance professional relationships by building a deeper level of trust and camaraderie. Middle managers should pay attention to the power of these informal interactions in creating a cohesive and supportive network.

Furthermore, middle managers need to maintain the relationships they build. This involves regular follow-ups, staying in touch through various means, and showing appreciation for the support received. Simple gestures like a thank-you note, a message of congratulations, or a check-in call can go a long way in maintaining solid relationships. Managers should also proactively update their network about professional developments and seek feedback and advice when needed. This continuous engagement helps in keeping the relationships dynamic and relevant.

Networking and relationship building are not just about professional gain; they also contribute to personal growth and fulfillment. The connections made through networking can lead to lifelong friendships, mentorship, and a broader understanding of the world. For middle managers, these relationships can provide a support system that helps them navigate the complexities of their role, offering advice, encouragement, and shared experiences.

Building a solid professional network is vital to a middle manager's role. It provides the support needed to tackle challenges, opens up opportunities for collaboration and growth, and enhances personal and professional development. By prioritizing networking, demonstrating empathy, maintaining consistency, leveraging diverse platforms, practicing reciprocity, and engaging in social interactions, middle managers can cultivate a network that supports their career aspirations and contributes to a thriving organizational culture.

Networking is more than a professional necessity; it is a pathway to continuous learning, innovation, and success.

Tool #14

Continuous Learning and Development

Encouraging A Culture Of Continuous Learning Ensures That Both The Manager And The Team Stay Updated With Industry Trends And Skills

The importance of continuous learning and development cannot be overstated for middle managers in the ever-evolving landscape of the modern workplace. Fostering a culture of ongoing education is crucial, not just for their own growth but also for the development and adaptability of their teams. This chapter explores how middle managers can encourage continuous learning, ensuring they and their team members stay abreast of industry trends and skills, ultimately driving the organization forward.

At the heart of continuous learning is recognizing that knowledge and skills are not static. The rapid pace of technological advancements, changing market dynamics, and evolving industry standards demand that professionals continually update their expertise. For middle managers, embracing this mindset begins with leading by example. When managers actively engage in learning, whether through attending workshops, earning certifications or simply staying informed about industry news, they set a powerful precedent for their teams. This visible commitment to personal growth demonstrates the value of learning and encourages team members to follow suit.

Creating an environment that supports continuous learning starts with fostering curiosity and openness. Managers can encourage their teams to ask questions, seek new information, and explore innovative solutions to problems. This can be achieved through regular team meetings where knowledge sharing is a crucial component. Inviting team members to present on topics they are passionate about or have recently learned about can stimulate interest and foster a culture of collective learning. These sessions enhance the team's knowledge base and build confidence and communication skills among team members.

Formal training and development programs play a significant role in continuous learning. Managers should advocate for and facilitate access to these opportunities. This could include enrolling team members in industry-specific courses, bringing in experts for in-house training sessions, or providing access to online learning platforms. By investing in these resources, managers signal their commitment to professional development and equip their teams with the tools they need to excel. Additionally, encouraging participation in conferences and industry events can provide valuable networking opportunities and exposure to the latest trends and best practices.

Feedback is another critical element in the learning process. Constructive feedback helps individuals understand their strengths and areas for improvement, guiding their learning efforts. Managers should create a feedback-rich environment where regular, meaningful feedback is provided and received openly. This involves pointing out areas for improvement and recognizing achievements and progress. A balanced approach to feedback fosters a growth mindset, where challenges are viewed as opportunities to learn and develop rather than setbacks.

Peer learning is a powerful yet often underutilized tool. Encouraging team members to learn from each other through peer mentoring, collaborative projects, and knowledge-sharing platforms can significantly enhance collective expertise. Peer mentoring programs, where more experienced team members guide and support their less experienced colleagues, can foster a supportive learning environment. Collaborative projects requiring team members to work together towards a common goal also promote sharing skills and knowledge. These interactions help to build a cohesive team that learns and grows together.

Leveraging technology is essential in today's digital age. Numerous online platforms offer many learning resources, from courses and tutorials to webinars and forums. Managers should curate and recommend these resources, making it easy for team members to access and engage with relevant content. Additionally, implementing project management and collaboration tools can streamline workflows and facilitate sharing knowledge and best practices. By integrating these technologies into daily operations, managers can create a seamless learning experience that aligns with the team's work processes.

Incentivizing learning can also motivate team members to engage in continuous development. Recognizing and rewarding those who actively pursue learning opportunities can reinforce the importance of this practice. This could be in the form of formal recognition during team meetings, career advancement opportunities, or even small rewards like certificates or badges. Managers can inspire others to invest in their learning journeys by acknowledging and celebrating these efforts.

Creating a culture of continuous learning has its challenges. Managers must balance the immediate demands of their roles with the long-term benefits of development. This requires careful planning and time management to ensure learning activities can be maintained alongside daily operations. Managers need to communicate the value of continuous learning to their teams, emphasizing how it contributes to personal and professional growth as well as to the overall success of the organization.

Ultimately, continuous learning aims to build a resilient, adaptable, and skilled workforce that can navigate the complexities of the modern business environment. For middle managers, this means fostering their own development and creating an environment where their teams can thrive. By prioritizing learning, providing the necessary resources, and cultivating a supportive and open culture, managers can ensure that their teams are well-equipped to face current and future challenges.

Continuous learning and development are vital components of effective middle management. By encouraging a culture of ongoing education, managers can ensure that they and their teams stay updated with industry trends and skills. This commitment to learning drives innovation, enhances performance, and positions the organization for long-term success. Middle managers who champion continuous learning advance their careers and play a pivotal role in the growth and development of their teams and the organization as a whole.

So, What Do You Do Now?

With 14 Tools Given To You, Will You Apply Them?

As we draw this journey through the Middle Manager *Manifesto to a close*, it's important to reflect on the pivotal role that middle managers play in the fabric of businesses and corporations. These individuals are not just unsung heroes but the backbone, bridging the gap between the strategic directives from the top and the operational realities on the ground. Middle managers ensure that organizational goals are not just translated into actionable plans, but also into tangible results, and that teams remain motivated and productive. However, in the current age of work, characterized by rapid technological advancements and evolving organizational structures, the traditional role of middle managers is under threat. Their days may indeed be numbered if they do not adapt and evolve with the times.

The need for middle managers to stay relevant has never been more critical. They can survive and thrive in this dynamic environment by embracing continuous learning, adopting new technologies, and developing a versatile skill set. This book has outlined fourteen essential tools that every middle manager should master to navigate the complexities of their role and prepare for potential advancement to upper management. Here is a quick summary of these chapters:

- **Effective Communication Skills**: Clear and concise communication channels are essential for bridging gaps between upper management and team members, ensuring that everyone is aligned with organizational goals.

- **Time Management Techniques**: Mastering time management helps in prioritizing tasks and ensuring deadlines are met without unnecessary stress, leading to increased productivity and efficiency.

- **Conflict Resolution Strategies**: Effective conflict resolution fosters a harmonious work environment and enhances team productivity by addressing and resolving disagreements constructively.

- **Team Building Activities**: Strong teams are built through trust and collaboration, leading to improved productivity and morale through activities that strengthen team cohesion.

- **Performance Evaluation Methods**: Regular and fair performance evaluations help in recognizing talent and addressing areas of improvement, thereby driving continuous development and motivation.

- **Decision-Making Frameworks**: Using structured decision-making processes ensures that choices are well-considered and beneficial for the team and organization.

- **Delegation Skills**: Effective delegation empowers team members, allows managers to focus on high-level strategic tasks, and fosters a culture of accountability and growth.

- **Motivation Techniques**: Keeping the team motivated ensures high performance and job satisfaction, contributing to overall organizational success.

- **Leadership Styles and Adaptability**: Understanding different leadership styles and adapting them to various situations helps in managing diverse teams and driving better results.

- **Feedback Mechanisms**: Constructive feedback fosters growth and improvement, both for the team and the manager, by providing clear guidance and recognizing achievements.

- **Crisis Management Plans**: Being prepared for crises ensures swift and effective handling of unexpected challenges, minimizing disruption and maintaining stability.

- **Resource Management**: Efficient use of resources minimizes waste and maximizes productivity, ensuring that the team operates at its best capacity.

- **Networking and Relationship Building**: Building a strong professional network provides support and opens up opportunities for collaboration and growth, enhancing both personal and professional development.

- **Continuous Learning and Development**: Encouraging a culture of continuous learning ensures that both managers and their teams stay updated with industry trends and skills, fostering innovation and adaptability.

As you reflect on these chapters, remember that the journey of a middle manager is one of constant evolution and adaptation. The skills and strategies outlined in this book are for surviving the present and thriving in the future. The work landscape is shifting, and those who can navigate these changes with agility and foresight will find themselves not only maintaining their relevance but also paving the way for future leaders.

For those aspiring to ascend to upper management, the path through middle management is unavoidable and invaluable. During this phase, you hone your leadership skills, understand the intricacies of organizational dynamics, and demonstrate your ability to drive results. The challenges middle managers face are opportunities to build resilience, adaptability, and strategic thinking—qualities that are indispensable at higher levels of management.

Moreover, as a middle manager, you have the unique privilege of mentoring and shaping the next generation of leaders. By sharing your knowledge, providing guidance, and fostering a supportive environment, you contribute to the growth and success of your team. This mentorship creates a lasting impact, ensuring that the values and skills you impart benefit the organization long after you have moved on.

In conclusion, while the role of middle managers is evolving, its importance remains steadfast. Embrace the tools and strategies presented in this book as your guide to navigating this dynamic environment. Whether your goal is to rise to the upper echelons of management or to excel in your current role, these insights will help you survive and thrive in the world of work. Your journey as a middle manager is a testament to your commitment to excellence, and with the right mindset and skills, you will continue to make a significant impact. Remember, the path to upper management is a growth journey, and every step you take as a middle manager brings you closer to achieving your goals. Keep learning, keep growing, and keep leading.

Research, Sources, and A Little AI Magic

How The Words In This Book Got Into This Book

I have said in more forums than I can even recall from memory how AI, specifically ChatGPT, has made me a better—and much more prolific—writer.

I have also said in almost as many places for even longer than I have hand access to AI tools that I am a sucker for tricks that add a few extra pages to my self-published books, which ensures I have enough pages in those books to make them thick enough to get the title and name printed on the bookbinding of the paperback.

I am presenting this chapter to list the sources from my research for this book. The book's overall theme and the focus for all the chapters is my original vision and the slow process of working on the best topical response. The design and flow of all the content is mine, with a little bit of filler, reorganizing, and grammar and spell checking from tools such as Wordtune, Grammarly, and the aforementioned ChatGPT. The bulk of the knowledge presented here may not be 'original thought-leader lore'—I didn't create any of it from whole cloth—but it came from lessons learned and content read and reviewed over my lifetime and career.

With that out of the way, I am also presenting these 64 links that were pulled as sources as I used the AI Tools to give more body to this boo to give the 'robot editor full credit for its assistance with this work. The links are listed alphabetically, with a brief description per their websites on who they are and what they do.

You may find somewhere in the list of 64 websites a new-to-you resource that will help you in your business or personal development progress:

1. http://2012books.lardbucket.org: Site for downloading Creative Commons Licensed Books

2. http://alertmedia.com: Helps organizations respond to critical events faster with the industry's most intuitive and powerful emergency communication solution

3. http://aprika.com: A team of experienced Project Managers and Salesforce Developers passionate about enabling better project management for Salesforce users around the world

4. http://birdviewpsa.com: A full-cycle platform aiding organizations in planning, managing, and forecasting projects, resources, and finances in one place

5. http://bryghtpath.com: Experience, tools, and partnerships to help your organization successfully navigate the rough waters ahead – and ensure your organization is prepared

6. http://business.expertjournals.com: An European peer-reviewed journal that publishes high-quality papers that are made available to worldwide audiences, through open access

7. http://careervillage.org: Mission is to democratize access to career information and advice for underrepresented people

8. http://ccl.org: A top-ranked, global, nonprofit provider of leadership development and a pioneer in the field of global leadership research

9. http://cipd.org: The professional body for HR and people development, championing better work and working lives for over 100 years

10. http://clockify.me: Helps hundreds of thousands of businesses across the world organize and run their business with the suite of products that include Plaky, Pumble, and Clockify

11. http://cmoe.com: Successfully partnered with organizations of all sizes and across

various industries around the world, with ongoing work and research within these organizations provides us with unique insights into the modern workforce

12. http://corporatefinanceinstitute.com:
    On a mission to enhance the skills, knowledge, and productivity of finance and banking professionals

13. http://cultureamp.com: Focused on building a new type of company: a company that truly puts culture first, that focus empowers our people to deliver on the promise of a platform that helps people worldwide build profitable, sustainable, and human-literate companies

14. http://ecampusontario.pressbooks.pub: Provides educators and learners with access to more than 1,600 free and openly-licensed educational resources

15. http://equalparts.co: Empowers the CEO and leadership team to make decisions, create cultural change, and maintain an efficient organization throughout growth and improvement

16. http://extension.uga.edu: Provides free, reliable, research-based information based on the latest scientific research in language that anyone can understand

17. http://fiercehealthcare.com: Delivers healthcare news at the intersection of business and policy, where ur journalists strive to bring our readers breaking industry news, exclusive interviews and thoughtfully-reported stories that offer a deeper insight on how changes in the industry impact their corner of the healthcare world

18. http://floowitalent.com: Reshaping the Future of Outsourcing for Rapidly Growing Companies, one Hire at a time

19. http://forbes.com: Forbes gives people the knowledge, resources, inspiration, and connections they need to achieve success

20. http://groupdynamix.com: Our mission is to "Connect People in Fun Ways," and our specialty is facilitating activities that improve relationships, increase collaboration and build team unity

21. http://hbr.org: Our mission is to improve the practice of management in a changing world, influencing how we approach what we do here and what we believe is important

22. http://hireborderless.com: A global payroll solution that leverages the power of generative AI to automate and speed up the process of on-boarding, managing, and paying international team members

23. http://hrcloud.com: Gives HR teams a new advantage over past approaches

24. http://hrmorning.com: Keeps you informed and prepared through weekly insights, tools, and training highlighting the most relevant HR topics, management principles and labor law changes

25. http://hubstaff.com: Clearing the hurdles between you & your goals

26. http://humaans.io: Building a new kind of employee management platform designed to help People Ops, Finance, and IT teams operate collaboratively

27. http://indeed.com: Our mission is to help people get jobs

28. http://intoo.com: Cares about the entire employee lifecycle, and our solutions are created to address the workforce needs of every organization, no matter the size, industry, or location

29. http://kincentric.com: By combining measurement and data-driven insights, we shape advisory solutions to help people and teams thrive at every level

30. http://lattice.com: The #1 AI-enhanced people platform that turns managers into

leaders, employees into high-performers, and companies into the best places to work

31. http://linkedin.com: The world's largest professional network with more than 1 billion members in more than 200 countries and territories worldwide

32. http://managementcenter.org: We get in our clients' business

33. http://managementisajourney.com: Helping you with the people side of the business™

34. http://manning.com: A publisher of computer books, videos, and projects for software developers, engineers, architects, system administrators, managers and all who are professionally involved with the computer business

35. http://mckinsey.com: To help our clients make distinctive, lasting, and substantial improvements in their performance and to build a great firm that attracts, develops, excites, and retains exceptional people

36. http://merrittbusiness.solutions: Your advocate, consultant, and we do the right thing for our clients, always

37. http://monster.com: A global leader in connecting people and jobs

38. http://neuroleadership.com: Over the last 25 years, we've cracked the code for culture change at scale, and you can discover what science-backed habit activation can do for your organization

39. http://online.champlain.edu: Founded as a career-focused business and accounting school in 1878, our history of getting students ready for success remains today. Wear your alma mater and its legacy proudly

40. http://paycom.com: Comprehensive payroll solutions to reward and reimburse employees

41. http://peoplebox.ai: Easily integrate goals and performance into people's workflows

42. http://planview.com: We help you translate strategy into business results for your most important initiatives and keep your organization and processes aligned

43. http://pmi.org: The global authority in project management, committed to advancing the project management profession

44. http://predictiveindex.com: We are a performance-based culture, and we expect a lot from each and every person we hire, so you're looking to coast, look elsewhere

45. http://projectmanagement.com: More than two decades of experience helping PMs improve their craft

46. http://quizlet.com: To give every student the tools and confidence to succeed, no matter what their motivation, or what they're striving to achieve

47. http://quora.com: To share and grow the world's knowledge

48. http://reflektive.com: Our experience with hundreds of organizations informs our approach and how we can help you get the results from performance management you deserve

49. http://researchgate.net: To connect the world of science and make research open to all

50. http://reworked.co: The world's leading community of employee experience, digital workplace and talent management professionals

51. http://riversoftware.com: We're ready to be your mentoring software and solution partner

52. http://smallbusiness.chron.com: Operates an active news bureau in Austin, ensuring its coverage taps directly into the heartbeat of Texas' legislative and cultural shifts

53. http://smartsheet.com: Creating innovative work management solutions, mobilizing a passionate and diverse global team, and making a positive impact in communities where we live and work

54. http://straightline.consulting: Leverage our unique abilities and focus on our client' strengths, always seeking to learn and grow

55. http://strategyblocks.com: We make it easy for organizations to succeed in strategic planning, strategy management and agile execution

56. http://structureddecisionmaking.org: An organized approach for working together to make informed and transparent choices in complex decision situations

57. http://teambonding.com: The leader in corporate team building activities for 25+ years

58. http://teambuilding.com: Brings these world class experiences together under one awesome banner

59. http://velocityokc.com: We help businesses succeed in Oklahoma City

60. http://voltagecontrol.com: A facilitation academy that develops collaborative leaders through certification programs for product

innovators, executives, consultants, and educators

61. http://wendyhirsch.com: Helping organizations and individuals master the art and science of change

62. http://wgu.edu: Goes beyond convention to identify, develop, and implement programs, systems, and technologies that pave the path to opportunity for all

63. http://womensforestcongress.org: A forum to develop strategies and solutions for forests through a female lens

64. http://worklodes.com: Draws on four decades of business experience to comment on the changing work experience

About The Author

J Cleveland Payne

J Cleveland Payne is a highly accomplished author, renowned entrepreneur, distinguished military veteran, and seasoned media professional who has significantly impacted various fields. With a genuine dedication to personal and professional development, Payne has established himself as a multifaceted individual with a remarkable passion for empowering others.

With over 25 years of experience in traditional radio and television broadcasting, Payne has honed his skills in delivering captivating content and engaging audiences. However, his contributions extend far beyond the realm of media. As the founder and operator of Fast Forward Business Properties, LLC, Payne is committed to providing top-notch personal and professional development training, helping individuals and organizations unlock their full potential. Through his expertise, Payne equips his clients with essential skills and instills the confidence to navigate the ever-changing business landscape.

In addition to his notable work in training and development, Payne spearheads More Better Media, LLC. This dynamic media production company specializes in creating compelling audio, video, and written content. Whether it be through thought-provoking podcasts, visually engaging videos, or informative written materials, Payne excels at crafting content that resonates deeply with audiences, leaving a lasting impact.

Payne's background as an Air Force veteran plays a pivotal role in shaping his commitment to excellence and ability to connect with people. His military service instilled in him invaluable qualities such as discipline, attention to detail, and a strong work ethic, all of which continue to influence his entrepreneurial pursuits and interactions with others.

Throughout his illustrious career, Payne has consistently demonstrated a steadfast dedication to continuous learning and growth. By embracing new technologies, staying updated with industry trends, and consistently exploring innovative approaches, he ensures that he delivers exceptional value to his clients and audience. His work as Operations Support Manager at Shorter College, a two-year HBCU in North Little Rock Arkansas, and as an Adjunct Professor teaching classes in Business and Entrepreneurship, is a testament to his commitment to empowering others and making a positive impact.

As a passionate advocate for personal and professional development, Payne strives to inspire individuals to reach their full potential, overcome challenges, and achieve their goals. His unique blend of experience in media production, training, and entrepreneurship, each field complementing the other, allows him to provide practical insights and guidance that are genuinely one-of-a-kind to those seeking personal and professional growth.

To connect with J Cleveland Payne and benefit from his wealth of knowledge and expertise, you can visit his personal website at jclevelandpayne.net or reach out to him via email at jclevelandpayne@gmail.com. His commitment to making a positive impact and empowering others is evident in his online presence and his dedication to sharing his insights with those who seek his guidance. He is always open to new connections and opportunities for collaboration.